Score
with
Basketball Math

Stuart A. P. Murray

Enslow Elementary

an imprint of

Enslow Publishers, Inc.

40 Industrial Road
Box 398
Berkeley Heights, NJ 07922
USA

http://www.enslow.com

Enslow Elementary, an imprint of Enslow Publishers, Inc.
Enslow Elementary® is a registered trademark of Enslow Publishers, Inc.

Library of Congress Cataloging-in-Publication Data

Murray, Stuart, 1948-
 Score with basketball math / Stuart A.P. Murray.
   pages cm. — (Score with sports math)
 Summary: "Learn and review math skills while also learning about the history of basketball"—
Provided by publisher.
 Includes bibliographical references and index.
 ISBN 978-0-7660-4178-3
 1. Arithmetic—Juvenile literature. 2. Basketballs—Juvenile literature. I. Title.
 QA115.M883 2013
 513—dc23
                              2012045291

Future editions:
Paperback ISBN: 978-1-4644-0295-1
Single-User PDF ISBN: 978-1-4646-1184-1

EPUB ISBN: 978-1-4645-1184-4
Multi-User PDF ISBN: 978-0-7660-5813-2

Printed in China
012013 Leo Paper Group, Heshan City, Guangdong, China
10 9 8 7 6 5 4 3 2 1

To Our Readers: We have done our best to make sure all Internet Addresses in this book were
active and appropriate when we went to press. However, the author and the publisher have no
control over and assume no liability for the material available on those Internet sites or on other Web
sites they may link to. Any comments or suggestions can be sent by e-mail to comments@enslow.com
or to the address on the back cover.

Design and production: Rachel Turetsky, Lily Book Productions

Illustration Credits: AP Photo/Keith Srakocic, p. 42; AP Photo/Michael Conroy, p. 38;
AP Photo/Michael Switzer, p. 40; AP Photo/Stacy Bengs, p. 44; Aspen Photo/Shutterstock.com,
pp. 17, 18; © 2012 Clipart.com, pp. 3, 5, 12, 16, 21, 31, 41; Domenic Gareri/Shutterstock.com,
pp. 4, 22; Photo Works/Shutterstock.com, pp. 7, 28; Richard Paul Kane/Shutterstock.com, p. 11;
Shutterstock.com, pp. 1, 41, 45; Wikimedia/*New York World-Telegram* and the *Sun* newspaper
photograph collection, p. 33; Wikimedia/&DC, p. 27; Wikimedia/Airman 1st Class, Daniel Hughes/
99th Air Base Wing, p. 34; Wikimedia/D. Gordon E. Robertson, p. 8; Wikimedia/Danny Karwoski,
p. 23; Wikimedia/Gary Denham, p. 13; Wikimedia/Jenspo, p. 20; Wikimedia/Jon Smith,
p. 14; Wikimedia/Reisio, p. 15; Wikimedia/saw2th, p. 26; Wikimedia/Steve Lipofsky,
www.Basketballphoto.com, pp. 25, 36; Wikimedia/Tim Shelby, p. 35; Wikimedia/Tulane
Public Relations, p. 6; Wikimedia/Verpacker Ing, p. 46.

Cover Photo: Shutterstock.com

Contents

NBA star LeBron James, left, fights for the ball.

INTRODUCTION
From Peach Baskets to "March Madness"

You probably know that basketball is played all over the United States and is becoming popular around the world. But did you know how much math there is in basketball? For instance, there are 2-pointers and 3-pointers, a 24-second shot clock, and players who make too many fouls are out of the game.

This is not to mention shooting percentages and a team's wins and losses. To have the most fun watching or playing basketball, you have to know math. In this book you will practice math and also learn basketball facts and history.

No dribbling allowed

When basketball was invented in 1891, the rules were very different from what they are today. For one thing, players were not permitted to dribble the ball. The ball was moved by throwing it to other players. And the basket really was a basket, the type used to pick peaches.

Every time there was a score, someone had to use a ladder to get the ball out of the basket. At first, that was not such a problem. In those days, teams scored very few baskets. The very first official basketball game ended with a score of 1–0!

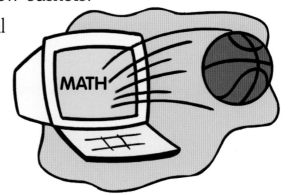

The game grows up

The rules soon changed, and dribbling was allowed. As the years passed, basketball became popular in many countries and was played in the 1936 Summer Olympics. In the United States, there were hundreds of professional basketball teams. They organized into leagues, and the National Basketball Association (NBA) started in the 1940s. By then,

Basketball is a leading women's sport.

most of the rules now in use had been set, and a "basket" earned two points. Today, almost every American middle and high school has basketball teams for both girls and boys. The NBA has 30 teams with stars earning millions of dollars. Many fans get most excited about the college championship. This tournament starts every March and is so thrilling to basketball fans that they call it "March Madness."

The NCAA Tournament

Basketball's college championship is run by the National Collegiate Athletic Association (NCAA). This tournament is one of the most important sports events in the United States. It starts with 68 teams that qualify by winning their leagues or by having the next-best records. These 68 play one another until only four undefeated teams are left: the "Final Four." These teams then play for the national championship.

College teams compete in the NCAA tournament.

1

"Basket Ball" Is Everywhere

Physical education teacher James Naismith is said to have invented basketball in the 1890s. Naismith taught future phys ed teachers in Springfield, Massachusetts. In the winter, his students needed an indoor game that would give them lots of exercise. Naismith nailed peach baskets at each end of the gym and made the first set of rules for "Basket Ball."

The new game caught on fast. Basketball soon was played in church gyms, high school gyms, and college gyms. Outdoor courts appeared on school playgrounds everywhere. Players' skills improved, and the best players brought out the fans.

The statue of basketball inventor James Naismith is at the University of Kansas, where he was on the faculty.

Small and crowded courts

When basketball was invented, gyms were small. They were designed for exercise, not for basketball. Most basketball courts were about 60 feet long and 30 feet wide. The first players were not allowed to dribble. They passed the ball up the court.

Q: A team moves the ball from the end line with two forward passes: 25 feet and 20 feet. A player shoots and scores. The court is 60 feet long. How long was the shot?

A: Add the two passes and subtract the total from the length of the court:

25 + 20 = 45 feet

60 – 45 = 15 feet

The shot was a 15-footer.

When basketball was invented in 1891, there were nine players on a team. Today there are five.

Q: How many more players were on the court in 1891 than today?

A: Add the number of players on each team:

9 + 9 = 18 in 1891

5 + 5 = 10 today

Subtract 10 from 18:

18 – 10 = 8 more players in 1891

Q: Basketball became an official Olympic sport in 1936. How many years did it take until basketball became an Olympic sport?

A: Subtract 1891 from 1936:

1936 – 1891 = 45 years

College players jump for the tip-off to start the game.

Passing to yourself

Early players could not dribble, but some would run and toss the ball in the air. They would catch it over and over. They were actually "passing" to themselves to move the ball up the court.

Q: **A player throws the ball in the air and catches it as he runs. He covers 30 feet of court in 10 steps. How many feet does he cover with each step?**

A: **Find the average number of feet per step by dividing 30 feet by 10 steps.**

$$30 \div 10 = 3 \text{ feet per step}$$

Baskets scored from play are called "field goals." Shots taken after fouls are called "foul shots," or "free throws." In early basketball, all baskets were worth only one point.

Q: **An early basketball game ends with the winning team scoring five times as many points as the losing team. The losing team has 12 points. What is the winning team's score?**

A: Multiply 12 points times 5:

12 × 5 = 60

The winning team has 60 points.

Q: How many total field goals and foul shots were scored?

A: Since all scores are worth 1 point, add 60 and 12:

60 + 12 = 72

The game had a total of 72 field goals and foul shots.

When free throws are taken no one is allowed to block the shot.

Basketball was a popular sport at the 2012 London Olympics.

Rectangles and hoops

A modern NBA court is a rectangle 94 feet long and 50 feet wide. These dimensions are much larger than the first basketball courts, which were in small gyms.

Q: An early basketball court's length is 60 feet. How many times would its length fit into an NBA court's length? Round to the nearest hundredth.

A: Divide 94 by 60:

94 ÷ 60 = 1.57 times

Q: The playing area of an old basketball court is 2,350 square feet. This is half the playing area of a modern basketball court. What is the area of the modern court?

A: Multiply 2,350 feet by 2:

$2,350 \times 2 = 4,700$

The modern basketball court is 4,700 square feet.

The basket is a round hoop 18 inches in diameter (wide). This is why the game is often called "hoops." Men's basketballs are about 9.4 inches in diameter.

Q: Estimate how much larger the hoop is than the ball. First, round the ball's diameter to the nearest inch.

A: 9.4 inches rounds down to 9 inches. The basket's rim is 18 inches.

Divide 9 into 18:

$18 \div 9 = 2$

The basket is twice as large as the ball.

The basket and the ball

Naismith put the baskets up high so that no one could stand in front and guard them. If the basket was down low then there could be rough play and injuries. The basket is 10 feet from the ground, but most NBA and college players can dunk the ball.

Q: How high does a player reach if his hand is 2 feet above the basket when dunking?

A: Add 2 feet to the basket's height, 10 feet.

2 + 10 = 12 feet high

Women's basketballs are about 9 inches in diameter (wide).

Q: How much smaller is the women's basketball than the men's (9.4 inches wide)?

A: Subtract 9 inches from 9.4 inches:

9.4 – 9 = .4

The women's ball is .4 inches smaller.

Q: If a 9-inch wide ball goes perfectly down the center of an 18-inch hoop, how much space is there around the ball?

A: First subtract 9 inches from 18 inches to find how much larger the hoop is.

18 − 9 = 9 inches larger

Imagine the ball as having two sides. There is an equal amount of space on each side, so divide 9 by 2:

9 ÷ 2 = 4½

There are 4½ inches of space around the ball.

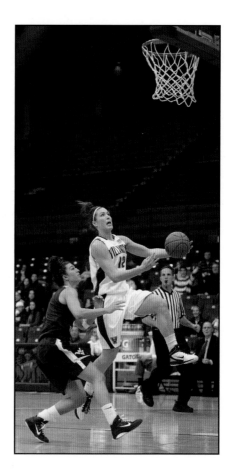

A college guard drives in for a layup after breaking away.

2

Offense:
Slick Passing, Jumpers, and Fast Breaks

For fans, good basketball can seem like two teams charging from one basket to the other. The ball is passed quickly. Guards dribble the length of the court on fast breaks and take jump shots. And forwards suddenly drive for layups.

Although it can go at high speed, offensive basketball is planned and practiced. Plays are run through in practice until everyone knows what he or she has to do. Teams work on offensive plays over and over. For every score that comes from a loose ball, a dozen baskets are scored from plays that have been worked on all season long.

Modern players can jump so high that they make dunks look easy.

Arcs, lines, boxes, and clocks

A major line on the court is the "3-point arc" in front of each basket. In the NBA, the arc is at least 22 feet from the basket. Field goals from outside the arc are worth 3 points. Inside the arc, they are worth 2 points. And at the top of the painted box called the "key" is the free-throw line. Free throws are worth 1 point.

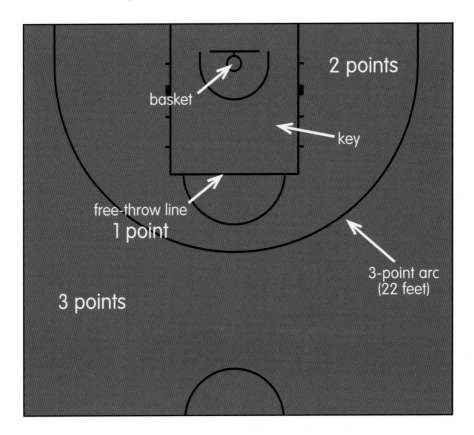

basket

2 points

key

free-throw line
1 point

3-point arc
(22 feet)

3 points

Q: At first the free throw distance was 20 feet. Today, it is ¼ shorter. What is today's free throw distance?

A: Divide 20 by 4 to find ¼ of the original distance.

$20 \div 4 = 5$

Subtract 5 from 20:

$20 - 5 = 15$

Free throws are now from a distance of 15 feet.

In the NBA, players have to shoot the ball within 24 seconds of their team getting the ball. First they have 8 seconds to bring the ball across the halfway line.

Q: A player dribbles the ball across the halfway line in 6 seconds. How much time is left to shoot?

A: The team has 24 seconds to shoot, so subtract 6 seconds from 24:

$24 - 6 = 18$ seconds left

Field goals and free throws

An NBA game ended with the winning team scoring 96 points. Half the winning team's points were 2-point field goals. One fourth of the points were 3-pointers.

Jump shots are often taken with a defender's hand close to the shooter's face.

Q: **How many of the points scored were from 3-pointers? How many 3-pointers were there?**

A: **Divide 96 by 4:**

$96 \div 4 = 24$ **points were from 3-pointers**

Divide 24 by 3:

$24 \div 3 = 8$ **3-pointers**

Q: **The losing team had ten 3-pointers, twenty-five 2-pointers, and fifteen free throws. What was its score?**

A: **Multiply 10×3 and 25×2, then add the products to the 15 free throws:**

$10 \times 3 = 30$

$25 \times 2 = 50$

$30 + 50 + 15 = 95$ **points**

Q: If a player makes 9 out of 10 free throws, what is his free throw percentage?

A: Divide 9 by 10:

$9 \div 10 = .9$

Add a zero for the hundredths place:

$.90 = 90$ percent

A player shoots 200 times during a basketball season and scores 80 field goals. Of these, 20 are 3-pointers.

Q: What is her field goal percentage?

A: It does not matter whether the field goal is a 2-pointer or a 3-pointer when figuring field goal percentage.

So, divide 80 by 200:

$80 \div 200 = .4$

Add a zero for the hundredths place:

$.40 = 40$ percent

Battles for the ball decide who wins or loses games.

The Greatest: Michael Jordan

Michael Jordan of the Chicago Bulls is said to be the greatest modern-day basketball player. In the 1987–88 season, Jordan was the NBA's most valuable player and also the highest scorer. He even won the NBA's defensive player of the year that season!

NBA 1987–88 Scoring Leaders

Player	G	FG	FT	PTS
Michael Jordan (Chicago)	82	1,069	723	2,868
Dominique Wilkins (Atlanta)	78	909	541	2,397
Larry Bird (Boston)	76	881	415	2,275
Charles Barkley (Philadelphia)	80	753	714	2,264
Karl Malone (Utah)	82	858	552	2,268
Clyde Drexler (Portland)	81	849	476	2,185
Dale Ellis (Seattle)	75	764	303	1,938
Mark Aguirre (Dallas)	77	746	388	1,932
Alex English (Denver)	80	843	314	2,000
Hakeem Olajuwon (Houston)	79	712	381	1,805

G (Games), FG (Field Goals), FT (Free Throws), PTS (Points Scored)

Use the scoring leaders chart to answer the following questions. The chart shows games played, field goals, free throws, and total points.

Q: Jordan scored 723 free throws. How many points did he score with field goals?

A: Subtract 723 from his total 2,868 points.
2,868 − 723 = 2,145 field goal points

Michael Jordan of the Chicago Bulls is considered the greatest-ever basketball player.

Q: How many more free throws would Dominique Wilkins have needed to equal Jordan's total points?

A: Find how many more points Jordan scored by subtracting Wilkins's total from Jordan's:
2,868 − 2,397 = 471 points
Wilkins would have needed 471 more free throws, which are worth 1 point each.

Q: From this table, can we tell how many field goals were 3-pointers and how many were 2-pointers?

A: No. That would require two more columns to show totals of 3-point and 2-point field goals.

The U.S. women, in white, defeated France in the 2012 Olympic basketball final.

Playing as a team

The U.S. women's basketball team has won the women's basketball Olympic gold medal seven times. In the 2012 Olympics, the women really did it as a team. They led all five team statistics: points per game, rebounds, assists, steals, and blocks. But no American led any of the individual player stats.

U.S. Women's Basketball Team:
Key Statistics in 2012 Olympics

Average points per game		Average assists per game		Average rebounds per game	
1 United States	90.6	1 United States	23.1	1 United States	50.5
2 Argentina	73.0	2 China	17.7	2 Australia	42.1
3 France	69.8	3 Australia	17.6	3 Russia	40.4
4 Czech Republic	69.0	4 Czech Republic	17.2	4 Czech Republic	40.0
5 China	67.7	5 Turkey	17.0	5 Great Britain	39.4
Turkey	67.7				

Q: The table shows three key stats: points per game, rebounds, and assists. Which team is in the top five as many times as the United States?

A: Czech Republic.

Q: How many teams are in the top five more than once?

A: Five, including the United States and the Czech Republic, China, Australia, and Turkey.

Q: How many teams made it into the top five in these stats?

A: Nine: United States, Czech Republic, China, Australia, Turkey, France, Argentina, Russia, and Great Britain.

The United States won first place in Women's Olympic basketball in 2012 by defeating France, which took second.

Q: The third place team also was third in assists: which team was it?

A: Australia, which defeated Russia.

The Australian women's team takes a time-out in their bronze medal victory over Russia.

3

Tough on "D"

Today's basketball players have amazing skills with the ball. They can dribble faster than ever and shoot from farther out. Their ability to jump for rebounds or to dunk has never been better.

Yet players of years ago had one special skill that modern players want to match: defense. For every basketball player, defense is difficult and exhausting. You have to stay with your opponent. You have to guess whether she is going to shoot or pass. And you must give everything you have to get the ball back.

The defender is ready for the guard's first move.

Fouls, steals, and blocked shots

Basketball players try not to foul. When they do, the other team usually gets a free throw. In early basketball, players had to leave the game if they made two fouls. As time passed, players were allowed more fouls.

Q: Today, NBA players are allowed three times as many fouls as early basketball players. How many fouls are NBA players allowed?

A: Early basketball players were allowed two fouls, so multiply 2 times 3:

2 × 3 = 6 fouls

On defense, players try to steal the ball, block shots, and get rebounds.

Q: A team has seven steals and four blocked shots—all inside the 3-point arc. How many possible points did they prevent?

A: Add 7 steals and 4 blocks:

7 + 4 = 11

Baskets scored inside the arc are worth 2 points.
So, multiply 11 times 2 points:

2 × 11 = 22 points

A center scores eight 2-pointers but also makes five fouls. The other team's free throws from those fouls score nine points.

Q: Did the center's scores earn as many points as the other team's free throws?

A: Multiply the center's 8 field goals times 2 points each:

8 × 2 = 16 points scored

Subtract 9 free throws from 16:

16 − 9 = 7

The center scored seven points more than the free throws earned.

$$\begin{array}{r} 8 \\ \times\,2 \\ \hline 16 \end{array} \qquad \begin{array}{r} 16 \\ -\,9 \\ \hline 7 \end{array}$$

Stats and championships

Bill Russell and Wilt Chamberlain were two of the greatest NBA players. The chart shows some of their best stats for a single season. It also shows how many NBA championships they won. Most of Chamberlain's stats were far better than Russell's.

Chamberlain's and Russell's Best Single-Season Stats:

	GP	MPG	RPG	PPG	NBAC
Chamberlain	82	48.5	27.2	50.4	2
Russell	81	45	24.7	18.9	11

GP (Games Played), MPG (Minutes Per Game), RPG (Rebounds Per Game), PPG (Points Per Game), NBAC (NBA Championships)

Q: Study the chart to see where Russell had a better stat.

A: Russell won more NBA championships.

Chamberlain was a great scorer, and Russell was a great defender. Russell's defense helped his teams win 11 NBA championships. Chamberlain's teams won 2 championships.

Q: How many times more championships did
   Russell win than Chamberlain?

A: Divide Russell's 11 wins by Chamberlain's 2 wins
   $11 \div 2 = 5\frac{1}{2}$ times

Q: How many times does Russell's season-best PPG
   go into Chamberlain's? First round to the
   nearest whole number.

A: 50.4 rounds down to 50, and 18.9 rounds up to 19.
   Divide 50 by 19:
   $50 \div 19 = 2.6$ times

Chamberlain was the top
NBA rebounder in 11 seasons.
But the chart shows that Russell
was almost as good a rebounder.

Q: How many more RPG
   does Chamberlain have
   than Russell?

A: Subtract Russell's 24.7 from
   Chamberlain's 27.2:
   $27.2 - 24.7 = 2.5$ RPG more

Superstars: Bill Russell, left,
played in the NBA from
1956–69. Wilt Chamberlain,
right, played from 1959–73.

Members of the 2012 U.S. men's Olympic team (l–r) Kobe Bryant, Carmelo Anthony, Deron Williams, Chris Paul, Kevin Durant, and LeBron James.

U.S. men win 2012 Olympics

The U.S. men's basketball team won the Olympic tournament for the third time in a row in 2012. They have earned an Olympic medal each time they have played: 14 golds, 1 silver, and 2 bronze.

Q: How many times has the men's team played in the Olympics?

A: Add the medals together:

14 + 1 + 2 = 17 medals

The team has played in 17 Olympics.

The players were all NBA stars. Some of them are on the chart at right. It shows their average minutes, rebounds, and points per game.

2012 Men's Olympic Basketball Leaders

Player	MPG	RPG	PPG
Carmelo Anthony	17.8	4.8	16.3
Kobe Bryant	17.5	1.8	12.1
Kevin Durant	26.0	5.8	19.5
LeBron James	25.1	5.6	13.3
Kevin Love	17.0	7.6	11.6
Chris Paul	25.8	2.5	8.3

MPG (Minutes Per Game), RPG (Rebounds Per Game), PPG (Points Per Game)

Q: One player was on the team because he was great at defense. Can you guess from studying the PPG column who he was?

A: Chris Paul was not a high scorer (8.3 PPG), so he must have been picked for his defense. (Paul was a four-time NBA All-Defensive Team player.)

Q: The highest RPG stat is more than four times another RPG stat. Whose stats are these?

A: Kevin Love has the highest RPG: 7.6. Multiply the lower RPG stats by 4 until you find the answer:

Kobe Bryant's $1.8 \times 4 = 7.2$

The best-ever Olympic team?

Some say the U.S. men's team that won the 1992 Olympics was the best team ever. It was called the "Dream Team." Others say the 2012 team was the best. Both were 8–0. The Dream Team won its games by an average margin of 44 points. The 2012 team won by an average of 32 points.

Q: About how many total points did each team win by?

A: Multiply their average winning margins times eight games played. For the Dream Team, multiply 44 by 8: 44 × 8 = 352 total points For the 2012 team, multiply 32 by 8: 32 × 8 = 256 total points

Larry Bird, left, and Magic Johnson, right, were among 11 future Basketball Hall of Fame players on the 1992 "Dream Team."

Kobe Bryant scores against Anthony Davis during a U.S. men's Olympic team workout.

Some say the Dream Team was better on defense. The 2012 team blocked 19 shots and stole the ball 83 times. The Dream Team made 47 blocks and 177 steals.

Q: How many more blocks and steals did the Dream Team have than the 2012 team?

A: Subtract the 2012 team's blocks and steals from the Dream Team's blocks and steals:

47 − 19 = 28 more blocks

177 − 83 = 94 more steals

4

The State Championship

Lincoln High has had its best basketball season ever. High-scorer Dylan Winfield, a junior, has led the team to the state final. Now they face Madison High. Madison has won the tournament the last two seasons.

Madison has a superstar, James Redpath, a senior. Dylan knows Lincoln has to keep James from scoring his usual 25 points a game—and from getting lots of rebounds. It will be a tough challenge.

Dylan is very good, but he knows if he cannot slow James down, Madison is sure to win its third straight championship.

A forward goes in for a layup as the defender tries to block.

The shooter gets fouled.

The first half

Dylan and James are both forwards, playing near the basket. On defense, Dylan will need Lincoln's captain, Jack Warner, to help guard James. The teams are ready for the tip-off. The ref throws up the ball, and the Madison center gets the ball to James.

Q: If Jack and Dylan both cover James, how many Lincoln and Madison players are left?

A: Subtract 2 players from Lincoln's starting 5:

5 – 2 = 3 players

Subtract 1 from Madison's starting 5:

5 – 1 = 4 players

It will be 3 Lincoln players against 4 Madison players.

Jack and Dylan cover James, but he still scores. In the first quarter Madison gets seven 2-pointers and two free throws. Dylan shoots three 3-pointers, and his team adds 4 more points.

Q: What is the score?
A: Multiply Madison's 2 pointers times 7 and add 2 free throws:
2 × 7 = 14 + 2 = 16
Multiply Dylan's 3 pointers times 3 and add 4:
3 × 3 = 9 + 4 = 13
The score is Madison 16–Lincoln 13.

$$\begin{array}{r} 3 \\ \times\,3 \\ \hline 9 \end{array} \qquad \begin{array}{r} 9 \\ +\,4 \\ \hline 13 \end{array}$$

The first half ends: Madison 35–Lincoln 32. Jack has three fouls. In high school basketball, if a player gets five fouls he is out of the game.

Q: How many more fouls is Jack allowed?
A: Subtract 3 fouls from 5 fouls:
5 – 3 = 2 fouls left

A very close game

In the second half, Dylan's scoring keeps Lincoln close to Madison. Jack finally fouls out trying to block James's shot. Without Jack it will be harder to defend against James.

Q: James had eight first-half points. Now he adds five 2-pointers and four free throws.

How many total points does he have?

A: Multiply 5 times 2 and add 4 free throw points:

$5 \times 2 = 10 + 4 = 14$

Next, add the 8 first-half points:

$14 + 8 = 22$ points

The defensive player goes for the block to try to stop the shooter.

Late in the half, the score is Madison 61–Lincoln 60. Dylan is tired, but he wants to win. By now he has scored seven 3-pointers and four free throws.

Q: **How many points has Dylan scored?**
A: **Multiply 3 times 7 and add four free throws:**
$$7 \times 3 = 21 + 4 = 25 \text{ points}$$

It is Madison 68–Lincoln 67 with 40 seconds to go. Madison inbounds the ball. They must get the ball across the center line in 10 seconds or they will have to give it up.

Q: **The Madison guard dribbles the ball for seven seconds. How many more seconds does he have to get the ball across the line?**
A: **Subtract 7 seconds from 10 seconds:**
$$10 - 7 = 3 \text{ seconds left}$$

The winning basket

The Madison guard passes the ball up the court toward James. But Dylan steps in and gets it. He takes off for the Madison basket. Then James gets in his way, and Dylan has to pass it off.

The offensive player tries to dribble around the defender.

Q: There were 31 seconds left when Dylan stole the ball. His team now uses up 20 seconds. How many seconds are left?

A: Subtract 20 seconds from 31 seconds:

31 – 20 = 11 seconds left

Lincoln is down 68–67. They have to shoot soon because the shot clock is running down. If they do not shoot, they have to give up the ball. Dylan sinks a 2-pointer.

Q: What is the score?

A: Add 2 points to Lincoln's 67:

67 + 2 = 69

Lincoln is ahead, 69–68!

With just 3 seconds left, James is calling for the ball. Dylan is right with him. The ball is in the air. James and Dylan jump for it! The final buzzer sounds, and the crowd roars! It is the Madison crowd cheering.

Q: James dunked the ball. What is the final score?

A: Add 2 points to Madison's 68:

$$68 + 2 = 70$$

Madison 70–Lincoln 69

Dylan is exhausted, but then James comes over to shake hands, saying, "You played a great game, man! Great game!"

Math Problem-Solving Tips

✎ Always read the problem completely before beginning to work on it.

✎ Make sure you understand the question.

✎ Some problems require more than one step to find the final answer.

✎ Don't think you always have to use every number in the problem. Some numbers are extra information and are not needed for the calculations.

✎ If you know your answer is wrong but can't find the mistake, then start again on a clean sheet of paper.

✎ Don't get upset! You can solve problems better when you're calm.

✎ If you're stuck on a problem, go on with the rest of them. You can come back to it.

A 1920s basketball.

Further Reading

Books

The Complete Book of Math, Grades 3–4. Greensboro, N.C.: American Education Publishing, 2009.

Connolly, Sean. *The Book of Perfectly Perilous Math: 24 Death-Defying Challenges for Young Mathematicians.* New York: Workman Publishing Company, 2012.

Fitzgerald, Theresa. *Math Dictionary for Kids: The Essential Guide to Math Terms, Strategies, and Tables.* Waco, Tex.: Prufrock Press, Inc., 2011.

Web Sites

Doina Popovichi. Math Basketball Games, 2010.

http://www.math-play.com/math-basketball.html
This web site offers games to supplement math lessons and make learning fun. Some of the basketball games are for either a single player or more than one player.

Kids Sports Printables, 2012.
http://www.printactivities.com/Theme-Printables/Sports-Printables.html
Here are printable sports worksheets and activity pages. These include math worksheets, counting mazes, word scrambles, and cryptogram puzzles.

Index